Un Your Amazing Memory

The Fun Guide
That Shows Grades 5 to 8
How to Remember Better
and Make School Easier

Brad Zupp

Simply Sensible Entertainment, Inc.

Unlock Your Amazing Memory - The Fun Guide That Shows Grades 5 to 8 How to Remember Better and Make School Easier

Copyright (c) 2013 by Simply Sensible Entertainment, Inc.
All Rights Reserved

Published in the United States of America by Simply Sensible Entertainment, Inc.
ISBN 978-0-9899547-1-6

Table of Contents

Chapter 1

Is This Book for You?

If you can answer yes to any of the questions, this book is for you.

- Are there any school subjects you dislike?

- Would you like to get better grades?

- Do you get bored during some of your classes?

- Do you study hard but forget the answers when you take a quiz, test or get called on in class?

- Does it take too long to study or do homework?

- Do you wonder how your friends can remember things so easily, and wish you could too?

This book will help. It contains simple, easy-to-understand tools to help you learn how to remember.

We are told, **"Remember this, it may be on the test."** But no one ever says *how* to remember.

All we are told is, "Just read it again!" But that is time consuming, boring, and doesn't always work.

It's frustrating. I know how you feel. When I was

Remember this, it may be on the test.

How?

younger, I had trouble with my memory. But I studied different techniques to learn what worked and what didn't, and my memory improved!

In this book I have taken techniques that are designed for adults and modified them for you. I have also created tools I wish I had when I was in school. If you read and practice the exercises, this book *will* teach you how to remember better! Remembering well *is* possible. If you can't already remember well, you are **not** dumb, lazy or worthless. Remembering better is a skill that *can* be learned!

Learning how to remember has many benefits.

By working through this book, you will:

- Finally know why you haven't been able to remember well.

- Learn how to get better grades, even in classes you don't enjoy.

- Learn a three-step process to remember anything and everything. People will respect you, your ability to remember, and how fast you learn.

- Learn how to use your creativity to make any subject more fun. It is easier to study the subject when it is enjoyable, which means better grades.

- Learn the best way to study and do homework.

We will go step by step together. You will use your creativity and probably laugh a lot. Read from the beginning. The book is organized to take you through the tools one by one in the right order.

Warning!

These methods may be different from what you've tried before. Give them a chance. I bet you'll be able to remember better by the end of the book - maybe even by the middle!

Before we jump in, here are some common questions:

? **Question: How hard is it to learn to remember better?**
Answer: It's easy. Like playing sports or games, the more you practice, the better and faster you will be.

Question: **Is it worth the time and effort?**
Answer: Definitely! Think about how much you have to learn each day in school. So much time is spent learning and remembering that it makes sense to learn these tools. It will save you a lot of time overall! It's like learning to ride a bike. It takes time, but it's worth it because of how fast you can travel on a bike compared to walking.

Learning memory tools requires some time at first, but is also worth it. You will remember information much faster and better after you read this book and try the experiments. *It's a skill that will last a lifetime!*

Easy but slow

Harder to learn, but faster

Question: I hate studying. Is this like having to study?
Answer: This is much different from studying. You use your imagination and creativity to think of funny pictures that are full of action and adventure.

Question: Why bother? I know I'm not smart.
Answer: You are **much** smarter than you think. Many people have discovered that by using memory tools, remembering is easy! They realize they are smart! By trying these tools, you will learn that you can remember better, faster, and make huge strides in school and life!

Question: I'm not motivated. Can you help?
Answer: We all feel unmotivated sometimes! Try this: use your imagination to picture what it would look and feel like to have a better memory. Imagine your friends being impressed, your family being proud, and your teachers being amazed. Can you imagine that? Those images are your destination. This book is your map.

Question: How does this work?
Answer: This book uses both the latest scien-
tific findings and tools that have been used for thousands of years. I have tried all the tools myself, and have helped many adults and students use them. They are effective. For now, learn the tools and practice them, and let the scientists worry about how they work!

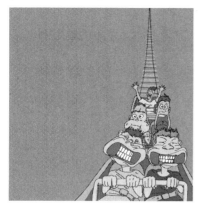

Ready? Climb aboard for an exciting ride and learn to unlock your amazing memory!

Chapter 2

All About Remembering: Step #1

What we call "remembering" is really three different steps.

Many people think of remembering as a one-time event, but there are three different steps required to "remember." Part of improving your memory is discovering which step is the hardest for you, then working at it until you see improvement.

The first step to remembering is to **get the information** by listening to your teacher or reading a book.

This step is the most important. More people trip on this step than the other two combined!

Here's an example: do you know what the 11th largest city in China is? No? Why not? Did you forget? No. You haven't *learned* it. You can't *forget* something you never *learned*.

There are times we try to remember something that we never *heard, read,* or *learned* in the first place. That doesn't work.

Have you heard the saying, "In one ear and out the other"?

It means hearing something and forgetting it right away. It goes in one ear, right through the mind, and out the other side. We think we forget, but we don't get the information.

The reason we often don't remember what we hear, see, or read is that we are often distracted, right when we should be focused! When that happens, we can't remember the information, because it went in one ear and out the other!

Our minds don't always realize that it's time to focus. We know we *should* be focusing, but for some reason we don't. Our friend whispers to us, or we think about being outside having fun. We need to train our minds to pay attention. By paying attention better, you will automatically remember better.

Have you ever heard, **"Okay, pay attention!"** Has anyone ever taught you *how*?

How to Pay Attention

Tool #1: The "No More Squirrel" Tool

If you ever feel that your mind is like a dog distracted by squirrels, this will help.

Read through the instructions first, then put the book down and practice this skill. You will be teaching your mind to pay attention and focus when you want.

First, sit up straight. This helps your mind stay focused.

Step 1: Close your eyes and breathe in and out through your nose. Take regular breaths, not too big or small.

After you breathe in and out, count. Do three full breaths (in and out is one breath), counting 1....2....3. Focus on any sound you can hear in your room during these first three breaths. Don't get distracted by it. Just notice the sound and keep part of your attention on it, while counting your breaths with the other part of your attention.

Step 2: Now count 1...2...3, one for each time you breath out. But this time, focus part of your attention on breathing and counting, and the other part on **the sound your nose makes breathing the air in and out**.

Step 3: Repeat steps 1 and 2. First, three in and out breaths, counting 1...2...3, and focus on a noise **in the room**. Then three breaths while focusing on **the sound of your breath in and out of your nose**.

If your mind wanders, that's okay. Just think, "My mind wandered away and thought about nachos" or whatever. Then focus on breathing, listening, and counting. Ready? Try it.

 Seriously - put the book down and try it!

What happened? Any of these?
- You got distracted: by sounds outside or your own breath.
- You're not sure what happened, but you lost track of the count.
- You started thinking about a bunch of other stuff.
- You did it easily. You kept track of the breath count and the sound you were focused on.
- You got sleepy.
- You didn't do it because whatever your excuse is.
- You felt like you teleported to a distant planet and had lunch with aliens.
- "Squirrel!"

Don't worry - these are all common reactions! (Well, maybe not the teleporting to a distant planet, but whatever you experienced is okay. You tried it, which is the most important part.)

"Squirrel!" Is your mind distracted and running loose?

Experiments have shown that this breathing tool helps train your mind to pay attention to **what** you want, **when** you want. By using this tool once or twice a day, for two rounds (or longer, if you can), you will improve your ability to focus. When your teacher starts talking, you will be better at directing your attention to what is being said. This helps with the first step of remembering: Get the information.

Tool #2: The "Guess What's Next" Tool

If you can keep your mind focused on what the teacher is saying, you will get more information. When you hear and see what is being taught, you will remember better. While listening to your teacher, try to guess what she is going to say or talk about next. Make it a game. This is another way to tell your mind, "Hey, pay attention! I may need to remember this later."

Tool #3: The "Count the Umms" Tool

Umm, we all use, like, helper words, ahh, when we're umm, talking, umm, if we aren't sure, umm, what we are, like, going to, you know, say.

Help your mind pay attention by keeping track of how many times the person you are listening to (your teacher) uses helper words. **Caution:** don't listen so closely for the umms and ahhs that you forget to pay attention to what the speaker is trying to **communicate.** Important: don't be rude and tell the person how many helping words they use. It's not polite, so keep it to yourself!

Tool #4: The "Ask Yourself How" Tool

When you are focused, you will hear things you need to remember. When that happens, ask yourself, **"How am I going to remember that?"**

When you ask yourself that question, your mind will focus even more. (By the end of the book, you'll be able to answer that question easily.)

Tool #5: The "One Activity" Tool

Do you dislike studying and doing homework? Do you try to have more fun by studying with the TV or computer on, texting, eating, listening to music, or everything at once?

Scientists have found that our brains can focus more attention by doing one thing at a time, and not by trying to do many things at once. It may sound boring, but focusing on **only** your homework (or studying) will help you remember better. You will also get it done faster!

Review of Step #1: Get the information

You learned several tools for focusing and paying attention. Without looking back, do you remember them?

#1: "No More _____"

#2: "Guess What's _____"

#3: "Count the ____"

#4: "Ask Yourself ____"

#5: "One _____"

Chapter 3

All About Remembering: Step #2

Once you have the information, make sure you keep it.

Now that you have improved your ability to focus, you are better at step one: get the Information. Now what?

Step two of remembering is: Save It. Save the information in your mind in an organized way to make it easy to remember.

Imagine wanting to wear your favorite shirt. If your closet or drawer is not organized, finding it may take some time (if you find it at all). Your memory is the same way. Organizing what you want to remember makes it easier to recall later.

There are three *keys* to storing information.

Let's look at them one at a time. Make sure you picture the color of each key. It will help you remember them later!

Key #1 is Green: Go "Picture It"

Change anything you want to remember into a silly picture.

Scientists have found that it is easy for the mind to remember pictures. To remember better, change the difficult-to-remember information into a picture. This converts the information into a format your mind is good at remembering.

Some information is easy to translate into a picture. To remember an ice cream cone, just picture an ice cream cone.

But what if what you need to remember isn't easy to picture? For example: you have to remember that President Buchanan was the only president from Pennsylvania, and many historians rank him as one of the worst presidents ever.

Picture It

Do you know what President Buchanan looked like? Me neither. Plus, I've been to Pennsylvania but I don't have a specific picture in my mind for it. And I've never seen the historians that rank him as one of the worst presidents, either, so that is also hard to picture.

If you can't easily picture something, ask yourself, **"What does it *sound* like?"**

President **Buchanan** sounds like 'blue cannon.'

The beginning of **Pennsylvania** sounds like 'pens.'

Next: the historians. If you can't think of anything it *sounds* like, you can also ask yourself, **"What does it remind me of?"**

Picturing historians ranking the president **reminds** me of judges on a TV show giving someone bad scores for his singing or dancing.

If you use your imagination to connect all these images, you might get a picture in your mind that looks like a blue cannon firing pens at judges.

Which is easier to remember, the original sentences about President Buchanan or the picture?

If this seems strange, or if you find the words easier to remember, don't worry! You may have to practice at first, but soon it will make remembering easy. Here are some guidelines for using the green key:

1. Decide what you want to remember.

13

2. Can you picture it? If so, create a mental picture of the fact or information.

3. If you can't picture it, ask yourself, "What does it sound like?" and "What does it remind me of?"

4. Be creative! Use whatever it sounds like or reminds you of to picture the information.

Here's a visual explanation of the "Picture It" process:

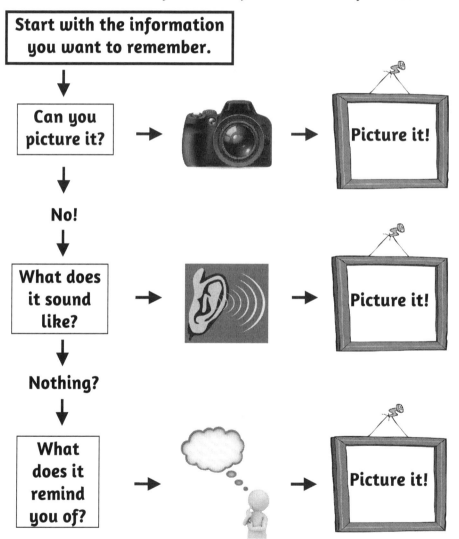

Use the process for a typical school problem: you are in class and need to remember details about the 8th president of the United States, Martin Van Buren.

Start with what you need to remember: **Martin Van Buren** was the **8th president** of the **United States**.

First part:

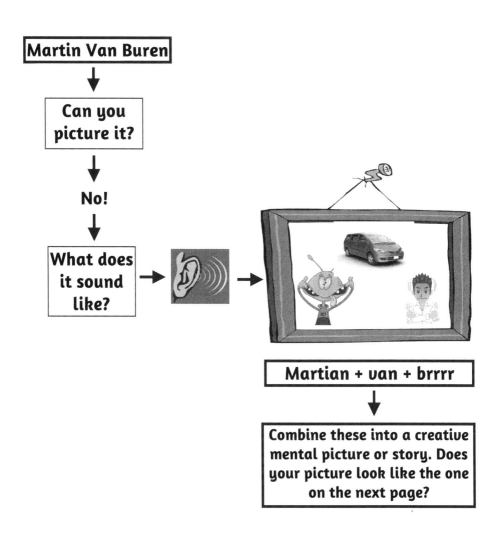

Martian + van + brrrr

Second part: Martin Van Buren was the **8th president:**

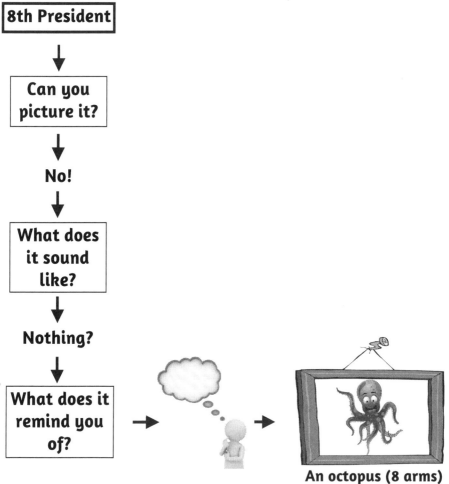

8th President

↓

Can you picture it?

↓

No!

↓

What does it sound like?

↓

Nothing?

↓

What does it remind you of?

→ → An octopus (8 arms)

When you combine the two images, you get:

Wait a second - what about **president** and **United States**? Why aren't they in the picture?

Our minds are like detectives from a TV show. All your mind needs is a few clues, then it can solve the case, remembering that Martin Van Buren was the 8th **president** of **the United States**.

If you are worried your mental detective **won't** be able to solve the case, you can always create another picture, and combine it with the rest of the mental image.

Can you picture the current president? Picture the **president** rescuing the van from the octopus, which adds **president** to the picture you already have.

Do you think the detective will remember that it's the 8th president of the **United States**? If not, add the president carrying a shield shaped like the **United States of America** to protect himself from one of the arms of the octopus, or whatever **your** memory creates. It's your mind, so create an image that is fun for you.

ESCAPE! Use *Interesting* Images!

Boring = Easy to Forget
Exciting = Easy to Remember

When you use your imagination to turn information into pictures, don't use boring pictures. Boring pictures are too easy to forget! The goal is to make information easy to **remember**.

For example, if you had to remember information about President Washington, you might remember what he looks like from his picture on the dollar bill. That is a good start, but it's boring.

Use the green "Picture" key and think, "What does **Washington** *sound* like?"

Washing/ton: washing sounds like washing machine, and **ton** sounds like a ton weight (like from a cartoon). Much better: two interesting pictures.

Now make your story picture exciting and memorable by adding **exaggeration, silliness, color, action, people** and **emotion**. If you take the first letter of each of these, you spell E.S.C.A.P.E. You want your images and stories to E.S.C.A.P.E. from being boring. Make them easy to remember!

Here is what the process looks like:

This is a more *memorable* way to picture President Washington.

That's an easy example, but some information seems impossible to remember *or* picture.

What about this? You are studying history and need to remember the date **1812**.

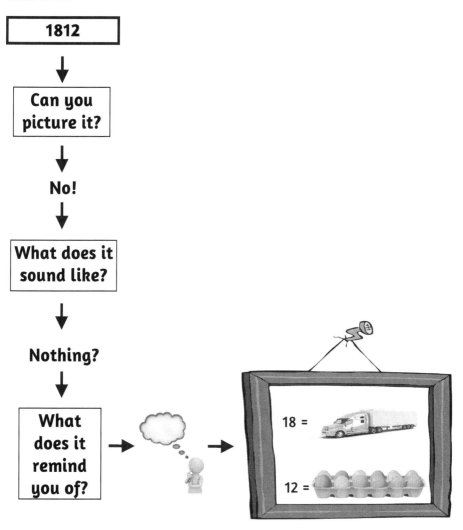

You get creative and think of an 18-wheeler and a dozen eggs!

Combine these two images.

> Use your imagination. Picture this funny story/image:
>
> A purple 18-wheel tractor-trailer with *huge* wheels and yellow racing stripes zooms down the road. Across all the lanes is a roadblock made of a crate of 12 gigantic red dinosaur eggs. The driver slams on his brakes but isn't able to stop in time. Egg shells and yolks fly everywhere as the truck crashes into them. The driver's face is dripping with egg yolks, and he's laughing at the mess he's made.

Does this picture E.S.C.A.P.E. from being boring?

- It has **exaggeration** (the tires and eggs are much bigger than in real life).
- It's **silly**. Why would there be a roadblock made of giant dinosaur eggs?
- It's **colorful**.
- There is **action**.
- There is a **person**.
- There is **emotion**. The driver is laughing at the mess.

Turning information into pictures can be a ton of fun. It makes even your least favorite subject more interesting to learn. Suddenly you're not trying to force yourself to remember information. You are picturing funny images or stories that make you smile. Be as creative as you can and remembering will be easy.

You now understand the first key: green means go picture it. Next, you need to *organize* information in your mind.

Key #2 is Yellow: "Connect It"

Connect images together
to organize them in your mind.

Scientists have learned that it is easier to remember new material when you can connect it to another piece of information you already know.

To use this memory tool, make a conscious effort to connect one image to another in a fun way. This works amazingly well when you connect a question picture with the answer picture. When you think of either one, you will think of the other because you will see the image or story in your mind.

In fact, you have already done it earlier in the book. Do you remember the information behind this picture?

If you are asked, "Who is the 8th president of the United States?" your mind detective will think of the key piece of information: **8th**. The detective will think, "What does 8 remind me of or sound like?"

You will probably *think* of the octopus. Then your detective will *picture* the octopus and solve the case.

As soon as you picture it, you tell your mind that the answer is connected to the octopus. Your mind knows that is where you have stored the rest of the information you need. You have organized the information. Your detective fills in the rest of the picture with the cold alien and spaceship that looks like a mini van.

Eventually, you will *know* the facts and won't have to picture them. The tools in this book help *as you learn new material*. You won't use them to remember a fact forever because your mind will eventually store the information for long-term.

This works... but don't just trust me! In the coming pages you will practice creating and connecting images into funny mental pictures, stories or movies using your imagination. You will *prove* to *yourself* that it works!

Here is the third and final key to unlocking your amazing memory. Have you guessed what color key this will be?

Key #3 is Red: "Review It"

Review the images and stories you create to make them even more memorable.

Scientists have discovered that when we think of something over and over, our minds form a type of pathway, like a path through the field or the woods. Walk on it enough and the path will be easy to follow.

It's why reading your notes or the textbook repeatedly *eventually* works, even though it takes a long time.

This key is used to review *your creative images*. Don't just re-read the information. Instead, review the information and *picture* the creative stories you invented.

Review It

? **Question**: If these keys are so helpful, why do I have to review? **Answer**: There are times you won't have to review at all (usually because the picture you imagine is so funny that thinking of it once will be enough to remember). There are other times the information is so easy you don't need to use the keys: you just *remember*.

Whether you need to review or not depends on: the information, how creatively you picture it, and how much you enjoy the topic. You decide: if you don't remember it easily, you need to review the story or image and even add more creativity (E.S.C.A.P.E.).

Review of Step #2: Save the Information

Congratulations! You have learned three keys and several tools for saving information. Without looking back, do you remember them?

P _ _ _ _ _   C _ _ _ _ _ _   R _ _ _ _ _

What does it
s _ _ _ _ **like?**

What does it
r _ _ _ _ _ **me of?**

E. _._._.A._.E.

24

Chapter 4

The Science of Reviewing

Understand the power of reviewing at the correct times.

Scientists have done studies that show how we learn - and forget. We start out not knowing much about a subject. Here's a graph of how it works.

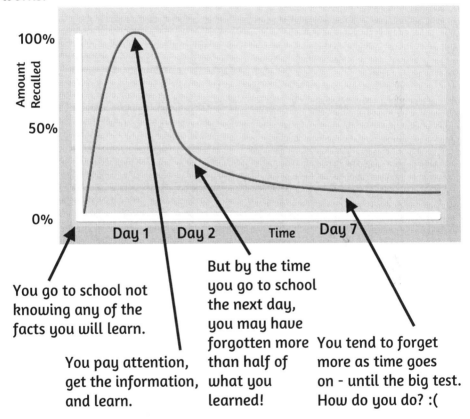

You go to school not knowing any of the facts you will learn.

You pay attention, get the information, and learn.

But by the time you go to school the next day, you may have forgotten more than half of what you learned!

You tend to forget more as time goes on - until the big test. How do you do? :(

DON'T PANIC! This is *normal.* Our brains naturally forget most of what we see, hear and learn each day, because we need to see, hear and learn more the next day, and the next.

The problem is that our minds don't know what we want remembered. You have to tell your mind, *"This is important to remember!"*

How? By reviewing.

Have you ever noticed how easy it is to remember the good things that happen to us? Or, sadly, the bad things too? We *review* those thoughts over and over, and our minds respond by remembering them. Your mind thinks, "This must be important. I will store this for long-term use." It's just like walking that path in the woods, making it easier to see over time.

For school work or other information you want to remember, you help your mind by reviewing *at the right times*. Scientists have found that by reviewing at certain times, our minds remember better. Here is the same graph as with the effects of reviewing added:

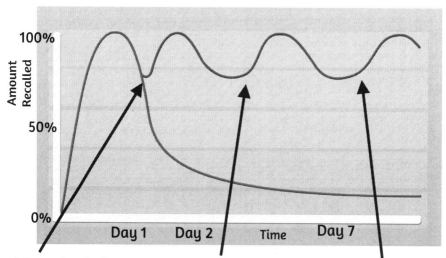

After school, do your homework! Review your notes and think about what you learned in each class.

Review again a few days later.

Reviewing at least once more will help further transfer it to long-term storage.

26

To remember better, you only need a few minutes of review *if you do it at the right times*. When you wait to do your homework, review your notes, or think about what you learned, you forget more and more. Even waiting until the next morning has a negative impact! Then you have to work extra hard so you can do well.

Use science. Try an experiment using this book. If you have an hour to read this book today, stop after 50 minutes. Close the book and think about what you learned. What are the key points? Review right away. Then, before you go to bed, review quickly again - just the key points. Picture them. How many can you remember?

When you wake up tomorrow morning, do it again. Next time you are ready to read, review what you learned this time, *then* start reading again.

Review in your mind every time after reading this book and you will better remember how to remember better.

Experiment to learn when reviewing works best for you. Review the new material each day - even if it's just thinking about it as you wash up before bed or eat breakfast in the morning.

Review one class or chapter on days 1, 3 and 5. Review a different one on days 1, 2 and 4.

Which do you remember better? Review your fun images and see which works best.

Most people review the same day, the next morning, and then the next night (two nights after first learning it). If it's difficult to remember, another review on day 4 or 5 helps.

Chapter 5

Creativity

Exercise your imagination to remember better.

These tools stretch your creativity.

? **Question: What if I'm not very creative?**
Answer: You are not alone. Some students say that the hardest part of this is creating silly pictures and stories. Here's how you can easily improve your ability to create fun and memorable images.

When you start to change the information into a picture, ask yourself:

- **What does it look like?** (Use this if it's easy to picture, like an ice cream cone.)

- **What does it sound like?**

- **What does it remind me of?**

When you have an *idea* for a picture, use **E.S.C.A.P.E.**

Take the basic image and ask yourself:
How can I **exaggerate** this? Can I make it bigger in my mind? Thinner, heavier, longer? (Don't make things smaller, because that makes them harder to see in your mind).

How can I make this **silly**? Can I picture it upside down? Curvy or straight? Lumpy? Melting? Oozing?

How can I make it more **colorful**? Use your *least* favorite color because it is memorable, or use colors that don't match.

How can I put **action** in it? Picture rolling, falling, flying, smashing into something, tumbling, or bouncing.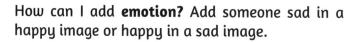

What **people** (or animals) do I know that could work in this picture? Does a friend or family member fit into the image? How about someone famous?

How can I add **emotion?** Add someone sad in a happy image or happy in a sad image.

You don't have to add every one. By adding two or more to your picture, it will **E.S.C.A.P.E.** from being boring.

Chapter 6

Play Time

Put these tools to the test.

Prove to yourself how fun and easy remembering can be.

Now that you've learned to use the tools, it's time to prove to yourself that they work in real-life situations. Some of the experiments will be easy, some may seem hard (at first).

Try them all. This is where you try the concepts. Knowledge is great but this fun practice will give you the ability to use these tools in your life.

Putting It All Together With Experiments

Experiment #1: State Capitals

At some point, we all learn the state capitals. For some people, these are easy to remember. Others find it hard. Many people find *most* of them easy and *some* impossible to remember. That's the way memory works. You may find it easy to remember the stats for your favorite sports figure, or lyrics to your favorite songs, but hard to remember dates in history, spelling or state capitals.

Whether the capitals are easy or hard for you, ***do not skip this section***! This same process is used to memorize world capitals and the counties of your state. So even if you know the state capitals already, review them using the tools!

Look at these examples to see how the keys are used. Do the activities: they are fun and will help you practice your creativity!

The old way to learn these would be to read a list of state capitals over and over and try to *force* your mind to remember them. Instead, let's use the *keys* and see how much easier it is.

Start with an easy one and use "What does it sound like?"

We need to connect two bits of information together: The capital of **Arkansas** is **Little Rock**.

Start with **Arkansas**. How can we picture that? Ask yourself, "What does it sound like?"

I think of "**Arrrr**" (what a pirate says) on a **can**. The ending is spelled "sas" but it sounds like "**saw**." I picture a saw.

Combine them in you mind. Does your image look like this?

32

Now connect it to "Little Rock." It's easy because it sounds like something we can picture: a little rock.

Next, connect or glue these two pictures together in your mind. See the pirate can hitting the little rock. What does it look like in *your* mind? Does the saw cut the rock into two pieces so the can/ship sails through? Does the can hit the rock and make a big hole? Does the pirate jump onto the island and bury his saw there? Make it interesting, creative, and fun. Imagine your own silly story or mental movie.

Even if you already know that Little Rock is the capital of Arkansas, don't skip this step. It's fun to create interesting mental images, and good practice for later when you learn information you don't know.

Sometimes it's hard to change information into a picture using "What does it sound like?" If you can't think of anything it sounds like, try using *"What does it remind me of?"*

Here's another one to practice.

The capital of **California** is **Sacramento**.

When I think of California, it reminds me of surfing. (So does Hawaii, so be careful - don't get confused.)

When I think of Sacramento, it *reminds* me of nothing! But is *sounds like* a grocery sack ("**Sac**") full of mints ("**ment**"). Can you picture a grocery sack full of mints surfing? A few of the mints fall out of the sack, and a shark eats them and has fresh breath! He even says "**Oh!**" because his mouth doesn't smell like fish any more.

Sack-mint-oh. It's not perfect, but your brain detective will follow the clues and figure it out.

You are giving your detective clues so later he or she can solve the case. You might think you need the "**ra**" sound, but usually your mind will figure it out. If you have trouble, though, add in the "**ra.**"

"**Ra**" reminds me of the noise that a cheerleader makes when cheering. If you add the image of a cheerleader, you get: Sack + cheerleader + mints + "oh!" (the shark).

Use your imagination and picture this funny story/image:

Picture a surfboard (which is how we're connecting to **California**) with a huge grocery sack on it. A cheerleader jumps out of the sack and does flips while staying on the surfboard in the waves. She is chomping on mints and even throws some to the sharks who smile with delight and say, "Oh!"

One more:
The capital of **Alaska** is **Juneau.**

When I think of Alaska, I think of a bear next to a beautiful lake with snowy mountains.

Then think of what **Alaska** *sounds like.* "**Al**" sounds like owl to me. I picture an owl asking ('**aska**') a big bear (reminds me of Alaska) who is cold and shivering if it's June yet. The bear is holding a calendar and trying to read what month it is. He is sad and confused because most bears aren't that good at reading. Or being able to tell what date it is. Poor bears!

Can you picture that, or can you invent something better?

? **Question: How does this work?**
Answer: When you need to recall the capital of Alaska, your mind will automatically try to think of the main points you know about the state: cold, beautiful, bears, snow.

Your mind detective then follows those paths, looking for any clues you many have left behind: the silly, colorful, active, exaggerated image of the bear and the owl. Your detective will fill in the rest and solve the case.

It works backwards, too. When you are asked what state **Juneau** is connected with, you will think that it sounds like the month of **June**. That makes you picture a calendar and warmer weather. Your mental detective then thinks of the bear holding the calendar, and links that to the owl flying and asking him a question. When you combine them, your mental detective remembers that Juneau is the capital of Alaska.

The capital of **Arizona** is **Phoenix**.
What do you think of when you think of Arizona? Do you already have a mental picture of a cactus? Or a desert?

Do you have a mental picture of the city of Phoenix? If not, have you heard of a mythical bird called a phoenix? It looks like a dragon.

How can you attach the phoenix to the cactus or the desert? Can you make a creative, fun, active, big, colorful image in your mind?

Do you remember the capital of **Arkansas**? What about the capital of **California**? Don't just remember the information. Think about your creative picture, like watching your favorite movie again, or re-reading a book. What do you *see*?

On Your Own

First, go through the list of states and pick two or three capitals you don't remember well. Second, **picture** the state and the city, then **connect** them in a creative way. Practice this now so it's easy, because the next section gets tricky.

Alabama - Montgomery
Alaska - Juneau
Arizona - Phoenix
Arkansas - Little Rock
California - Sacramento
Colorado - Denver
Connecticut - Hartford
Delaware - Dover
Florida - Tallahassee
Georgia - Atlanta
Hawaii - Honolulu
Idaho - Boise
Illinois - Springfield
Indiana - Indianapolis
Iowa - Des Moines
Kansas - Topeka
Kentucky - Frankfort
Louisiana - Baton Rouge
Maine - Augusta
Maryland - Annapolis
Massachusetts - Boston
Michigan - Lansing
Minnesota - St. Paul
Mississippi - Jackson
Missouri - Jefferson City

Montana - Helena
Nebraska - Lincoln
Nevada - Carson City
New Hampshire - Concord
New Jersey - Trenton
New Mexico - Santa Fe
New York - Albany
North Carolina - Raleigh
North Dakota - Bismarck
Ohio - Columbus
Oklahoma - Oklahoma City
Oregon - Salem
Pennsylvania - Harrisburg
Rhode Island - Providence
South Carolina - Columbia
South Dakota - Pierre
Tennessee - Nashville
Texas - Austin
Utah - Salt Lake City
Vermont - Montpelier
Virginia - Richmond
Washington - Olympia
West Virginia - Charleston
Wisconsin - Madison
Wyoming - Cheyenne

With these tools you can have fun making up creative, silly, and colorful images with the material. You are a movie producer, artist, cartoonist, photographer and animator all rolled into one.

When you need to **review**, read the information again quickly, picturing those unique images that make you smile.

Does it seem too easy? Too hard?

Too easy

These are simple tools that help you remember. They are easy, and that's fine. Easy can be good! *Don't ignore or discount them because they seem "too easy."* Use them and see your grades improve.

Too hard

If you're having trouble, it's probably for one of two reasons. Either:

1. You have difficulty translating the information into pictures. It takes practice to figure out what the information reminds you of, or to break down a word or idea into pieces that sound like something you can picture.

Solutions:
• Stick with it. Work on "What does it sounds like?"
• Don't be too literal. Aim for silly, wild, unreal or strange.

For example, remember **Alaska**? Does "al" really sound like "**owl**?" Not really, but it *kind of* does. Expand your thinking. Make bigger leaps in your imagination. It doesn't have to sound *exactly* like what you need to translate. Just make it *close*! Instead of **al**, how about **ala** = alakazam: a magician with a magic wand?

The last part: "**ska**." Could you change that into "**ski**?" **Ala-ski**: a magician skiing down a mountain in **June**, (not much snow) yelling "**ohhhh**!" They are *your* images, *your* imagination. If Alaska reminds you of a big purple pumpkin for some reason, picture that. Make the pictures your own, and have fun.

2. You picture the information but can't *remember* the pictures because you aren't making them silly, fun or creative enough.
Many people have this problem when they first start. If they have to picture a chair, they imagine a normal chair.

Solutions:
• Exaggerate! The easiest is way to imagine everything *huge*.

• Use E.S.C.A.P.E. Ask yourself how you can make the picture bigger, sillier, or more interesting. How can you add action, people, or excitement and emotion? Instead of just imagining a chair, imagine the best chair ever, the King of chairs! That is a memorable image.

Chapter 7

Memorizing the World

Your imagination is amazing!

Powerful tools make even the hardest facts easy to remember.

Experiment #2 - World Capitals

Did you skip the state capitals? Try these *world* capitals. You will get another chance to see the tools in action and practice your memorizing skills.

Start with an easy one:

The capital of **Netherlands** is **Amsterdam**.

"**Never**-Never Land" from *Peter Pan*? A **hamster** ("**Hamsterdam**") running across a huge **dam** holding back water? Is the hamster running to fix a hole in the dam to save Peter Pan and the city of Never-Never Land?

That is the picture my imagination created. What did *yours* create?

The capital of **Ethiopia** is **Addis Ababa**.

Wow, this might be difficult. You will be faced with many words or concepts that seem impossible to remember at first. Just relax and use the keys. Green Key: "Picture It."

What does it remind you of? Nothing? What does it sound like? Still nothing? Uh oh.

Break it into smaller pieces. Start with *one letter*: **E**. In my mind, "E" always reminds me of **elephant**. Elephant starts with E, and is easy to picture. To start picturing Ethiopia, use the first letter and picture an elephant.

That leaves "**thiopia**"? "**Thi**" sounds like "**tea**" that you drink. So picture an elephant drinking a huge cup of tea through its trunk.

"**Op**" in the middle of the word sounds like "**hope**," and then we're back to an "**eee**" sound, which can be another **elephant**. The last sound is "**ah**."

Make this funny story/image as silly as you can:

Put them all together: an elephant drinking tea from a large cup sprays the tea into the mouth of another elephant who was hoping to get a drink. The second elephant says "Ahhhh" with his mouth open wide for another drink.

That's a lot of effort for **Ethiopia**. This image takes a few seconds to create in your mind, but is memorable once you picture it.

• **Don't get discouraged.** Your ability to break words into smaller pieces will get better and faster as you practice, just like you get better and faster at any sport or activity you practice.

• **Timing is everything.** At times it makes sense to use these tools, and times it is better to just try to remember something by reading it once or twice. Stay tuned, we'll discuss this soon. For now, picture what I create, or use *your* imagination instead.

The next part: **Addis Ababa** is the capital of **Ethiopia**. When I say Addis Ababa out loud, the first thing I think of ("What does it sound like?") is a **baby** ("**a baba**"). I see a baby.

"**Addis**" sounds like "**add**" so I picture a giant **calculator**. Combining them, I imagine a baby using a calculator.

Connect that to the elephant picture of Ethiopia. Can you imagine that? I picture the baby sitting on the back of the first elephant adding up how much water is being squirted into the other elephant's mouth. To make it more interesting, maybe you can picture the baby sitting in the tea cup.

That mental movie is **exaggerated, silly, creative** and has **action**. Change the **color** of the elephants to make the image better. Add some **emotion**: the baby is concerned that all the drops of tea will be gone and he won't be able to take his bath! Now you have every part of E.S.C.A.P.E.

An easier one: The capital of **New Zealand** is **Wellington**.

New Zealand is where some of *The Lord of the Rings* movies were filmed. Use "What does it remind me of?" instead of "What does it sound like?"

Connect the hobbit to a well (a hole in the ground that supplies water) that has a cartoon 1-ton weight falling into it. Splash! I bet your hobbit is drenched! In your imagination, how does the hobbit feel about that?

Feel your creativity improving? If you want to learn all 194 countries, you *can*, and it would be a fun challenge. It is easy if you use the keys to unlocking your amazing memory.

Review Time

Think of the creative pictures you imagined.

What is the capital of New Zealand?

What is the capital of Ethiopia?

What is the capital of Netherlands?

What is the capital of Alaska?

What is the capital of Arkansas?

What is the capital of Arizona?

What is the capital of California?

If you found any of these difficult, review them, making sure to E.S.C.A.P.E.

Chapter 8

Vanquish Vocabulary Troubles

Creativity is the key.

Dread vocabulary no more. Now it's easy.

Experiment #3: Vocabulary Words

No matter what grade you are in, you have vocabulary words to memorize. These are going to seem easy compared to the world capitals.

Since many different ages are reading this book, some of these words might be too easy for you. If you already know a word, just skim it to see how the keys are used, then try the process with a word of your own.

Empathy (noun): **experiencing the feelings, thoughts, or attitudes of another.**

You know how this works now. Connect **empathy** with **experiencing the feelings, thoughts, or attitudes of another**.

What does empathy sound like? To me, Em= **M&M candies!** **Path** = a **path** to follow. Picture a path of M&Ms through the woods. E.S.C.A.P.E. - add a person you know who loves candy. Add emotion: she is hungry, running along the path, looking for M&Ms and eating them.

Connect that image to the definition. **Feel** yourself experiencing her **feelings (hunger)** or **thoughts: "Where do these M&Ms go? Who put them here? Should I be eating food off the ground? Are there bears in these woods? Do bears like chocolate?"**

Connect with her attitude (**"I'm so cool to have found these!"**). Picture watching her and picture yourself **experiencing** her feelings, thoughts or attitudes.

Neutral (adjective) **Staying away from either side of an argument.**

New troll? New-tray-owl? Connect one of those (or create your own) to the definition. I picture two people arguing about who gets to keep the new troll. They are pulling it back and forth and are almost breaking it. They turn to you because they want you to decide who gets to keep it, but you shake your head because you don't want to take either side of the argument.

Create a fun story involving your best friends (which adds emotion, because if you take one side the other will be mad at you). E.S.C.A.P.E. What colors can the new troll be? Action? People? Emotion? Done, done, and done.

Shrill (adjective.) **Having a sharp, high sound.**

Shhh and **drill**. A librarian is telling people who are drilling holes in books to be quiet because they are making a sharp, high sound (like the noise a dentist drill makes).

Get the idea? I bet you are becoming an expert!

What if you have to remember which words are verbs, adjectives, or nouns? You might know from the word itself, but you can always imagine a specific picture for verb, adjective and noun, and connect it to each definition.

All you have to do is create an image for verb, adjective, and noun. Then put that image into the picture for the word and definition.

One way is to use the *first letter* of each part of speech: **v** for **verb**, **a** for **adjective**, and **n** for **noun**. When you need to remember whether it's a noun or a verb, you'll remember the creative mind movie of the definition, and also see a part of the image that doesn't belong - that will be the part of speech.

For example:
V = vampire (or vegetables, vulture, or whatever you create)
A = alien (or apple)
N = nachos (or nut, or nurse)

Example:
Shrill: fit an alien into the story in the library. Is the librarian actually an alien?

When you need to remember anything, the first thing to do is ask yourself, *"How can I remember that?"* Then use the steps (Picture, Connect, Review).

Are you seeing that remembering can be much easier than you thought? Your mental detective is grateful for the extra clues you are leaving.

? **Question: When should I use these techniques?**
Answer: Use these techniques when have trouble remembering a word, subject, detail or any other fact. *These techniques take a few extra seconds.* It would take too much time to use them to remember *everything*. If you can look at your vocabulary words (or any other facts) and remember most of them, that's great! Move on to the next page or next subject.

Use these techniques when you struggle with a fact, the spelling of a word, or even an entire school subject. If you have tried to remember a fact two or three times and aren't able to, use these techniques. They will help you turn hard-to-remember information into pictures that are so fun there is no way to forget them.

Chapter 9

Spectacular Spelling

Spelling made silly.

Nevir mispell dificcult werds agin.

Experiment #4 - Spelling

From early in school we are asked to spell correctly. Can we use the same keys to remember how to spell words? Absotively, posilutely!

We often remember how to spell *most* of the word except for one place we get mixed up. For example, there are *double* letters in the middle of a word but we think it has a *single* letter. Other words are spelled with "**E**" but we spell them with "**A**."

The following examples teach you how to use the tools, *not only* how to spell these words. So even if you *know* how to spell the word, read the explanation!

Which is spelled correctly? Calendar, calander, or calandar?

Most people have trouble with the vowels in words like this. Ask yourself, **"How can I remember the correct spelling? How can I remember the part I mix up?"**

The proper spelling is cal**e**ndar. The vowels are "**a**," then "**e**," then "**a**." Ask yourself, "How can I remember **a, e, a** for **calendar**?"

Picture. Connect. Review.

Picture a calendar. Don't picture a boring one! E.S.C.A.P.E.!

Now picture **a/e/a**. You might think of an **a**lien **e**ating an **a**pple and finding a calendar rolled up inside the apple. Or *picture* flipping through the calendar for the first three months: January/February/March.

Find a way to remember the order of **a/e/a** and *connect* it to **calendar**. Leave some clues for your detective to find later.

Remember using an **e**lephant to start picturing **Ethiopia**? You were using the Alphabet Images. Remember when you first learned the alphabet? Each letter had a picture connected to it to make the letters easier to learn and remember. Use the same idea to spell better. When you have a picture for each letter of the alphabet, spelling is much easier.

The Alphabet Images

A student had trouble remembering how to spell the word **uncle**. Once she learned these tools, plus the Alphabet Images, she spelled it correctly every time, because she remembered this picture: her **uncle** is carrying an **u**mbrella and it's raining **n**achos. The nachos attracted a **c**ow that ate the nachos, while the uncle had to scare away a **l**ion that was carrying a hungry **e**lephant. Both the lion and elephant wanted the nachos, but the cow had gotten there first. I hate it when that happens.

The chart on the next page has suggestions of pictures for each letter. Look them over or make up ones that are more memorable for you, then practice the spelling words (or use your own, but *get creative!*).

A = apple, ant or alien	N = nut, nachos or nurse
B = banana or bee	O = orange or octopus
C = cookie or cow	P = pizza, pineapple or puppy
D = donut or duck	Q = queen, quesadilla, quiche
E = egg or elephant	R = rice or rabbit
F = French fries or fish	S = soda, syrup, snail or squirrel
G = grapes or giraffe	T = taco, tea, toast or tiger
H = hamburger or hippo	U = unicorn
I = ice cream, eye or *me* ("I")	V = vampire
J = juice box or jaguar	W = waffles, watermelon, whale or wolf
K = kiwi fruit or kangaroo	
L = lemons, lasagna or lobster	X = x-ray
M = marshmallows, muffin or monster	Y = yo-yo
	Z = zebra or sleeping "zzzzzzz"

Here is a word that confuses many people. Which example is spelled correctly: comittee, committe, or commitee?

There are many words like that: commit, committed, commitment, dessert and desert. How in the world can we remember them all? One "T" or two? Who decided to make this so difficult? One "T" here, two there, remember this word has two "M"s but one only one "T"... There has to be a better way!

For the earlier example, the correct spelling is **committee**. Ask yourself, "How can I remember that committee has *two* "M"s, *two* "T"s, and *two* "E"s?" What clues can you leave behind for your detective?

If you know that committee means "a group of people formed for a specific purpose," you could **picture** a group of six people meeting around a table. (Just so you know, this is just an example; a committee can have fewer or more than six people.)

Picture the six people split into three pairs, all arguing with one another. That gives your detective the clue that there are *three pairs of letters*.

Not enough clues? Break it down, but still use the keys.

Even if you don't know the meaning of a word, you can still create a picture. **Committee**. "What does it sound like?" *Picture*: **Comb** + **mitt** (baseball mitt or mitten) + **tee** (t-shirt or the tea you drink).

What else do you need to remember? The spelling: that there are *two* "**M**"s, *two* "**T**"s, and *two* "**E**"s. With all this material, it should be easy to create an interesting image or story.

Connect these two stories into a big picture or movie. Be creative. E.S.C.A.P.E. (*Exaggerate*, make it *silly*, *colorful*, filled with *action*, *people*, and *emotion*.)

Use the Alphabet Images for any letter combinations that are difficult to remember. Here are some other words to practice.

Acceptable, accidentally, accommodate

If these were your spelling words, the first question would be: can you remember how to spell each of these, without much effort? If so, great. Next! Move on to other words.

If you can't remember them perfectly, use the tools. Ask yourself, "Which part of the words do I misspell?

Do you have a problem remembering if there are two "**C**"s? If so, make a picture for the two "**C**"s, and connect that picture to the word's meaning (or what the word sounds like, if you don't know the meaning).

Make the information that is difficult to remember easy to remember using creative pictures. (Aliens find two **cows acceptable**, **accidentally** beam them up and **accommodate** them in the spaceship?)

You can also use the sound of the word to picture it. Say "**acc**" out loud - like **acceptable** and **accommodate**. It has always reminded me of the sound a cat coughing.

Can you picture an **acceptable cat,** or an **accommodating cat**? Even picture a **cat** having an **accident** on the carpet!

If you created a different picture for "**acc**," use that. No problem. Connect it to each word. Simple and effective. When you spell the word, you will think of the cat coughing, and you'll think of "**acc**."

What if you are having trouble spelling the rest of the word, too? What do you do? You know by now. The same process: picture it, then connect it.

Picture the **acceptable cat** and a **table.** You know how to spell table, so connect the cat to the table: you'll know both the two "**C**"s and how to spell the end of the word.

Picture the **accom̲m̲odating cat** eating two M&M candies.

Give your mental detective the clues it needs to make you an excellent speller.

Occasion, **occurred**.

C is for cookie! I would much rather have *two* **cookies** instead of one, especially at the **oc̲c̲asion** of my birthday! And it never **oc̲c̲urred** to me not to eat *both* cookies, even though I could have given one to each of my *two* **r̲a̲bbits**.

If you often forget that there are two letters together, like in **occasion**, change those two letters into pictures and picture *two* of them interacting with the word. If you often forget that there is only one letter, instead of two, picture *one* object, person or animal interacting with the word. Make sure the picture is clear that there is only one of the item you are imagining.

If there is a vowel (like an "**A**") that you often mistake for an "**O**" or an "**E**," translate the correct letter into a picture (like an ant or apple) and connect that to the picture of the word.

Here are some other examples of how being creative helps with spelling and vocabulary:

Antarctica and **arctic**.
Which one is on "top" of the world, and which one is on the "bottom?" Antarctica is on the bottom. How could you picture that **A̲n̲tarctica** is at the bottom of our planet?

Desert and **dessert**.

I'd like more **des̲s̲ert** - in fact, I'd like *two*, please! When you think of having two desserts, your mind detective uses that clue to remember that dessert is spelled with two "**S**"s.

Defense and **fence**.

They *should* be spelled the same, except for "**De**" in front of one, right? No can do, my friends. You need to remember that **defense** has an "**S**" and **fence** has a "**C**".

Use your alphabet images for "**S**" and "**C**." Connect one to a sports team playing **defense** made up of all "**S**" players (snails?). Connect your "**C**" alphabet image to a fence (cows sitting on a fence?).

You should know the process by now. When you need to remember information, ask yourself these questions:

• Which part is hard to remember? How can I change that into something I *can* remember?
• How can I picture it?
• What does it sound like?
• What does it remind me of?

Then **Picture. Connect. Review.**

This last spelling technique alone may help you get amazing grades.

Old MacDonald Had a Farm

You've heard "**I** before **E** except after **C**," right? If only that was always true! Along come the *weird* exceptions. The ones spelled with "**EI**" instead of "**IE**."

A tool to remember words that are spelled "**EI**" is to think of the old song about Old MacDonald: "**E I E I O**." Since Old MacDonald had a farm, picture "**EI**" words and connect them to the farm or Old MacDonald.

Here are several examples to picture:

Weird: Picture Old MacDonald with a weird hairstyle, or a friend of yours with weird clothes living on a farm.

Reign: Imagine a king reining over the cows and chickens.

Seize: Create the image of the police seizing all of Old MacDonald's chickens because they are too big.

Height: See a giant Old MacDonald measuring the height of his huge chickens.

Chapter 10

Never Forget Foreign Languages

Make friends worldwide.

Use memory tools to learn more words faster.

Foreign languages are easy if you are good at translating words into pictures using "What does it sound like?"

Using memory tools to remember foreign languages helps bridge the time between learning the words and knowing them well. The goal is to use the tools on the words that are challenging, or to learn words more quickly than could be done without the tools.

Rules for remembering foreign languages:
1. If you want to speak it correctly, you must memorize the word based on how it *sounds*.
2. If you want to spell it correctly, you must memorize the word based on how it is *spelled*.
3. The spelling and pronunciation are often completely different items to memorize.

4. Pretend each word is an English word you haven't learned yet. There is nothing dramatic about a different language, so don't let your mind stress you out!

You know how to learn new words. Apply the same techniques you have practiced to these words, and relax!

1. Learn how to say the word in class, on a CD/sound file or from a person who speaks the language. (If you have a text book that shows you how to correctly pronounce a word, you can use that, but be careful not to memorize the wrong pronunciation.)

2. Ask yourself, "What does it sound like?" or "What does it remind me of?"

3. If it doesn't sound like something, break it down by syllable, or into a word that sounds close enough to give your mental detective a clue.

4. Make a fun picture of the foreign word.

5. Picture the meaning or English word.

6. Combine the pictures of the two words into a story. Then connect the two words together in a fun, creative way.

There are only a few examples here, because you should learn the correct pronunciation in class or otherwise hear it before memorizing. Use the techniques on the language you are learning, and the experiment below as practice for your class.

Experiment #5 - Foreign Languages

The process works for any language:

Gato = **cat** (Spanish)
Gato is pronounced like "got toe," which is an easy way to picture it. Connect a cat to "got toe."

Japanese Examples

Neko = **cat** (Japanese)
Neko is pronounced like "neck oh." Picture the cat jumping onto your neck and you exclaiming, "Oh!"

Iku ("Ee kuu") - **to go**
Even though it is pronounced "ee kew," to me it sounds like "**eek! ew**!" Could you picture getting so excited about going somewhere that you say "**Eek! Cool!**"? Picture that. Give your mental detective some good clues.

Suki desu ("Ski dess") - **I like it**
Skiing on **desks**? Sounds like something **I like**. Picture that.

French Examples

Tout ("too") - **all, every**
Sounds like toot without the final "**T**." See yourself playing **every** horn that makes a '**toot**' sound.

Ca me plait ("Sa may play") - **I like it**
Picture a **saw** that might (**may**) **play**. When he does, he likes it!

We could go on with different words in many languages, but you know how to do it yourself. Find a friend, neighbor or classmate who speaks a different language. Ask them how to say words you can easily picture, like car, house, frog, happy.

Practice changing their language into pictures that can be connected to your mental pictures of common objects.

Before you know it, you will know many words in another language, and you will have proven to yourself how easy it is to learn and remember languages.

Chapter 11

Beyond Question & Answer

Connecting everything to anything.

Expand your ability to organize information.

There are times when you can't connect what you want to remember to a question or word. For example, it's your teacher's birthday tomorrow, and you want to remember to wish her happy birthday when you first see her in the morning.

You need to turn her birthday into a picture you can easily remember. Then you have to connect it to - what? That's right - connect that picture to *her*.

How? Picture a birthday cake with many candles burning.

E.S.C.A.P.E. Picture a *huge, ugly, spinach* cake with stinky cheese frosting and hundreds of candles. Mmmmm, yummy. What a delicious **desert**. Or is it **dessert**? (Do you remember which is correct?)

> What does your imagination create to connect your **teacher** with **birthday**?

How can you link it to her? Make up a fun picture or story in your mind about the cake. Do the candles burn so much she has to use the fire extinguisher to put them out? Is she tripping and about to fall onto the cake? Use your imagination to connect the image you selected for **birthday** to the image you have of **her**.

When you see her the next day, your mental detective will look at her and remember the silly story, helping you to remember to say "Happy Birthday!"

What if you keep forgetting your chore of taking the trash out at your home? Your family is disappointed, you feel bad, but you can't seem to remember to do it. How could you possibly remember? (You may not like doing chores, but allow me to teach you how to remember them, so you can keep your family happy.)

Following the keys, you'd picture the garbage can, then connect it to the front door to remind you to check it right when you get home. You could then review the silly image to help remember.

How can you use E.S.C.A.P.E to picture the garbage can and connect it to your door? Picture a huge garbage can, with a silly shape, in a color you dislike. Add action: flies buzzing, or thousands of ants crawling. Emotion: your family feeling embarrassed at how messy it is and angry that you forgot... again.

When you get home, your memory detective will remind you when you get to the door - *if* you E.S.C.A.P.E. and make the picture interesting enough.

You can connect what you need to remember to people, houses, your classroom, or anything you want. It's important to choose the correct item, place or person to connect to your other image.

If you need to remember to take the trash out, you might be tempted to connect the trash can image to yourself. That wouldn't be as effective as the door, the kitchen, or even the big trash barrel outside, because you would probably not think of yourself when you walk into the house.

You could connect it to your mom, because she could be upset if you forget again. That would work if you see her *before* you have to remember the trash. To trigger the memory and make your mental detective go to work, you have to see at least one clue. If your mom picked you up from school, you might remember when you saw her. But you might forget again by the time you got home. So connecting the image to the door is best.

How would you remember to take out the trash on a certain day of the week? When you think of Wednesday, what comes to mind? A TV show you enjoy? Picture that. Halfway to the weekend? Picture one half. What does Wednesday sound like? **Wed** sounds like a **wedding**. Picture getting married in the middle of a pile of trash because you forgot to empty the trash can. Sorry, dear!

Make sure you pick your connecting image carefully so it will give your mental detective the clue it needs at the right time.

Connecting Many Items
Tool #1: The Story Method

You need to remember lists of items at times in school, especially in math and science classes. There is a method to remember many items in a row. This concept makes learning much easier.

The basic idea is to make up a story that makes sense *in order*. You connect multiple items in a row to one main item. You have already read and practiced this.

Remember how my student remembered how to spell "**uncle?**" Her uncle (main picture) was holding an umbrella while nachos fell from the sky like rain onto it. A hungry cow started eating the nachos. The uncle had to make a lion, who was carrying an elephant, wait to eat. The cow had gotten there first.

This is a favorite method of many people, because it is fun and easy. Each image is connected to the one before it in a fun way. (Some people call this the **Link Method**, because each story is like the link of a chain or like linking paperclips together.)

Connecting Many Items
Tool #2: The Memory Castle
(Oh, that sounds cool!)

There is another way to organize your memory for a list of items you need to remember or a group of facts that are related.

The tool is called the Memory Castle or the Journey Method. If you live in a castle (or a regular home), there are many rooms that you know well. You know your castle so well that you could even walk around in the dark and not run into the furniture.

Imagine using each room of your castle to organize images. You could save a funny picture of a cold Martian flying a mini van spaceship in your bathroom, with the octopus reaching out of your sink or tub to grab the spaceship van. Can you picture that happening in your bathroom?

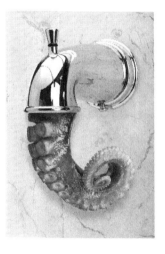

Using rooms in your castle to store information may be easier than the Story Method. Some people prefer to connect or link stories together, while many people find connecting stories to a location to be much simpler. Try both and see which you prefer.

The concept is: first, just like before, translate what you need to remember into pictures. Then, connect those pictures *to a location* that you have previously selected, like a room in your home.

Experiment #6 - The Kitchen Memory Castle

Using the picture of the kitchen below and the grocery list:

1. Create an exaggerated, funny image for each grocery item.

2. Attach each image to its location (#1: milk gets creatively connected to the top of the refrigerator).

1. milk connects to the top of the refrigerator (sour & forgotten behind the plant)

2. cereal connects to the inside of the refrigerator (soggy and saved for later)

3. ice cream connects to the microwave (heating it up)

4. eggs connect to toaster (don't "make them fit"!)

5. bread connects to sink (wet, mushy bread... yummy!)

6. cookies connect to blender (cookie crumbs for the ice cream)

7. carrots connect to stove top (a garden growing on the stove means your family doesn't cook often)

8. oranges connect to inside of the oven (they were on sale - now the oven is stuffed full)

When you need to recall the grocery list, you mentally walk through your "castle's" kitchen and see each of the locations you picked out. The items you connected should jump out at you - if you made up fun images.

A grocery list is not what you are normally asked to remember, though, is it? Don't worry, this tool can be used for school just as easily.

*Experiment #7 - **Your** Memory Castle*

Let's create a memory castle to learn a different list of items: **chicken, pizza, cow, car, butterfly**.

Look around the room you are in now or imagine a favorite room in your home. Picture yourself standing in the main doorway of the room. What is the most interesting thing in the room near the door to the left, in the corner? Call that **location #1**. Connect an exaggerated **chicken** to that item.

Look to the left of that area and/or object. What is along the wall? A lamp, a doorway, a plant, desk, or bookshelf? Whatever it is, connect **pizza** to **location #2** in a creative way using E.S.C.A.P.E.

Continue going around the room in the same direction. Look at a wall, then the corner, next wall, next corner, third wall, third corner, fourth wall, fourth corner. Pick the most interesting, memorable item near each. Use the ceiling (**location #9**) and the floor (**location #10**) as the last two locations to store (connect) pictures.

Connect **cow** to **location #3**, then car to **location #4**, and butterfly to **location #5**. Don't be boring. Exaggerate.

Congratulations! Your room has become a memory castle where you can organize your memories. When it is time to remember each object, mentally walk around the room and "see" what is where.

To create more journeys or memory castles, here are some suggestions:
1. Always go around every room the same direction so you're never confused. Most people go clockwise from where they start.

2. Start at the doorway of each room, every time. That makes it easy to remember the starting point when you have many rooms for memory storage.

3. Corner-wall-corner-wall-corner-wall-corner-wall then *ceiling* and *floor* is a great sequence for almost any room. This gives you 10 storage places to hold images. You can call them locations, file folders, cubbies or whatever you want. I call them locations or journey points.

What can be used as a location to store images? Any place you can picture well. If you can take a mental walk through the place and picture what comes next, it can be a place to store information.

• Start with rooms that are familiar to you. Your room, your kitchen, the bathroom, outside your home.
• An easy 26-location journey is the Alphabet Images you learned earlier. Connect whatever you need to remember to Apple, Banana, Carrots, Donuts, etc.
• Your favorite shopping mall. Think of all the unique stores where you could organize information to remember.
• Each classroom where you need to remember a series of information or facts. They don't have to be stored in order. **This tool works to help remember groups of related facts too, in order or not.**
• Do you have a favorite movie or TV show? Use the rooms or locations as a journey.

This is how memory athletes (like me) store the order of long numbers and memorize shuffled decks of playing cards. It also works for speeches, poetry or random words.

? **Question: Building memory castles sounds like *a lot* of work. Do I really have to do this?**

Answer: You probably don't need more than one or two good memory castles for storage locations. But it's safer and more reliable to use the Memory Castle method. If you use the Story Method to remember a long list or a bunch of similar facts, and forget one part of the story in the middle, you risk forgetting everything that comes after.

Experiment #9: Memorize the List of Presidents

If you want to impress your friends and family, translate each president's name into a fun image (remember Martin Van Buren?), then use the Memory Castle Method to store images. You can quickly memorize the presidents, in order, forwards, backwards and by number.

Chapter 12

Numbers: There Are So Many of Them

Remembering numbers can be surprisingly easy.

Every day we have to remember numbers. Dates, phone numbers, prices, addresses and more. Some people find numbers hard to remember because they are abstract. Memory techniques to the rescue! The memory keys make it simple and easy to remember anything, including numbers.

In school we need to remember numbers mostly for math and dates in history. Math is important for everyday life, so it's very important to be able to do math well and remember numbers.

This is the same process as remembering spelling, vocabulary and foreign languages. *Don't skip ahead.*

The first step to remembering numbers is to figure out a memorable, creative image for each number, *in advance.* Some people create these images based on "What does it sound like?" Some use "What does it remind me of?" and others combine both. It doesn't matter which system you use, as long as you can easily picture an image for each number.

The next step is to combine the numbers into a story.

The last step is to combine the number with the other information you need to remember (question and answer) You can also store the image of the number in your memory castle.

Focus on the first step. Here are images that work well for me. Try these for now. If they don't work for you, you can change them later *after* you've learned the method. Use any image that reminds you of the number, whether it's a *person*, *action*, *object*, or a combination of all three.

0 = Looks like a *soccer ball*. (Use any image that reminds you of soccer: *soccer player* or *kicking*.)

1 = Looks like a *baseball bat*. (Use *player*, *swinging bat*, *baseball*.)

2 = Reminds me of pair of *shoes*. (I see a *ballerina* wearing *dancing shoes* and *kicking* her leg up.)

3 = Reminds me of a *tricycle*. (Think of a *child riding* a *tricycle*.)

4 = Four legs remind me of a *chair*. (A *business person leans back* in a *chair* and starts to fall!)

5 = Looks like a fish hook. (A *fisherman catches* a *fish*.)

6 = Ants have six legs. (Ants can also *carry* objects bigger than themselves... like a *watermelon?*)

7 = Looks like a *boomerang*. (See a *kangaroo throwing* a *boomerang*.)

8 = Eight legs equals an *octopus*. (Should be easy to *juggle crabs* with 8 arms!)

9 = Looks like a *lasso* a *cowgirl* would use to catch a *cow*.

If you have trouble remembering dates or big numbers, it makes sense to spend a few seconds using the keys to unlocking your amazing memory.

Example: 1969 was the year the United States put a man on the moon.

Picture the **moon**. Connect the moon to a **baseball bat** (1), **lasso** (9), then **ant** (6), and finally another **lasso** (9).

Think of a **baseball player lassoing** an **ant** (1, 9, 6). For the last number, I think of the ant **lassoing** (9 again) the **moon**, which ties everything together.

Experiment #10: Master Numbers

Put it all together. Use any combination of the images that remind you of each number, as long as it makes sense to you both when you think of it *and* when you recall. The only "right" way is however *you* are able to remember the number.

Can you break the code and figure out the four-digit number?

Figure out the story (number) from left to right.
What number is linked to ballerina? _
What number is connected to kicking? _
What number is like a tricycle? _
What number is related to cow? _
This picture creates which number?   _ _ _ _

How did you do? Did you get the date of 1974? No? That's good, because the *correct* answer is 2039.

Can you use the code to *create* a four-digit number?
(Oh, *and* connect it to a historic event?)

1929: Wall Street crash (stock market), start of the Great Depression.

1 (baseball bat) + 9 (cowgirl) + 2 (shoes) + 9 (cowgirl)
Connect the image to Wall Street crash. What can you create with your imagination?

I would picture a baseball player (**1**) lassoing (**9**) a ballerina (**2**) who is standing on top of a cow (**9**) while sad-looking people (**depression**) sit on a **wall** running through the middle of **street** into which cars are **crashing**.

Using your imagination to make fun images that will be easily remembered by your mental detective! It may take some practice, but it's worth it. Suddenly, remembering numbers is *much* easier.

Pick out dates that are required in your class and see how easy (and fun) it can be to remember numbers.

 ## Dates with Months and Days

To remember dates that include months and days, you need a picture for each month. (You already have a system to remember days of the month, by combining the numbers from 0 to 9 to make the date.)

Think about a system to remember the months. You could use the images you already have for numbers 1-9 for January to September, but you would have to create new images for October (10), November (11) and December (12).

October reminds me of Halloween.

November reminds me of Thanksgiving.

December reminds me of Santa Claus.

(You could also take a few minutes to think of a holiday and image for each month, instead of using your numbers (1-9) for January through September.)

September 17th, 1787: a convention of delegates approved what would become the U.S. Constitution.

September 17, 1787 equals 9 + 17 + 1787, creating several pictures to connect. Use the Story Method, or consider the Memory Castle (your history classroom) as a way to organize the pictures.

My image would be a cowgirl (9 for **September**) swinging a baseball bat (**1**) at a boomerang (**7**). I would place that in a location, then in the next location picture a baseball player (**1**) throwing crabs (**8**) at a kangaroo (**7**). The kangaroo hops into a room where people in old time clothes are giving the thumbs up to a piece of manuscript. But that's me. What is your memorable image?

Chapter 13

All About Remembering: Step #3

Once you get the information and save it, make sure you recall it!

The **third** and final **step** to remembering is to **recall** the information. Thankfully, recall happens nearly automatically once you get the information and use the keys to remember it. Your mental detective is always on the search for clues.

Watch out! There are some villains that try to defeat you and your mental detective on your quest to recall well.

The Villains That Make You Forgetful

The Stressanator

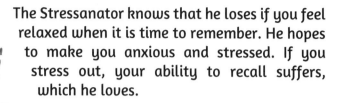

The Stressanator knows that he loses if you feel relaxed when it is time to remember. He hopes to make you anxious and stressed. If you stress out, your ability to recall suffers, which he loves.

The best way to defeat The Stressanator is to breathe and relax. Here's how.

The Relaxation Breathing Exercise

Read all the instructions first.

Close your eyes or look ahead. Release any tension in your shoulders.

Breathe in and out through your nose slowly two times.

Next, breathe in through your nose. When you breathe out, make your out breath longer than your in breath. It doesn't have to be exact. Just try to breathe out longer than in. Breath this way for 30 seconds or a minute, letting go of any thoughts. If anxious thoughts enter your mind, breathe and let them go.

The Tired Tyrant

The Tired Tyrant is as mean as The Stressanator, and twice as sneaky. His knows that when you are tired, you focus less, think more slowly, and don't remember as well.

The Tired Tyrant is hard to fight the day of a test. It is best to avoid him from the start. Get to bed early the night before a test.

Plan to sleep in 90-minute increments, which is how long most people need for a full sleep cycle. If you can schedule your alarm for the end of a sleep cycle, you will wake up more refreshed.

How many hours would you sleep if you didn't use an alarm clock? Try to sleep that many hours every school night, even if it means going to bed earlier than you think is cool.

Scientists have done studies showing that for every extra half hour of sleep a student gets, reading level, mood and attention all improve. Imagine being smarter just by sleeping more. Defeat The Tired Tyrant while snoring!

If you are under age ten, scientists suggest 10 to 12 hours of sleep a night. Are you 11 or 12 years old? Get ten hours at least. A teen? Nine hours are a minimum.

This is one of the easiest ways to improve your memory. Go to bed fifteen minutes earlier each week until you have reached the right amount of time for your age and needs. Then watch your grades improve!

Another way to defeat The Tired Tyrant is to eat a healthy breakfast. Skipping breakfast robs your body and mind of fuel, but *feeds* The Tired Tyrant. He gets stronger while you get weaker (mentally and physically). Don't let him win.

The Energizer Breathing Exercise

If you are tired, this breathing exercise helps you wake up and focus. Do it in private as it's noticeable to people around you.

Breathe in and out through your nose, very quickly, breathing not just from your lungs, but from your diaphragm in your stomach area. Breathe three short quick breaths per second. It sounds and feels like you are a dog trying to sniff out a scent.

Try this for 10-15 seconds. Don't do too much the first several times you try - you might get lightheaded! Practice when needed to wake yourself up and feel energized.

Fear Man

Fear Man feeds on fear. He loves making you think of all the *awful* things that *could* happen. Fear Man is related to The Stressanator, and **the Relaxation Breathing Exercise** defeats him, too.

Your second line of defense is to visualize yourself taking the test or answering the questions you are asked. See yourself answering the questions correctly. *Feel* that you know the answers. (Don't review the answers while visualizing: feel what it will be like to *know* the answers.) Picture yourself happy and proud. Breathe and relax as you do this. You will feel and do better.

Mr. Overexcited

Mr. Overexcited seems so cute and harmless. Who doesn't love to be excited about something?

Have you ever seen a big sporting event where the teams were well-prepared and confident but still performed poorly? They weren't stressed or afraid. They were visited by Mr. Overexcited and he robbed them of some of their skills.

A visit from him doesn't feel bad, but he can hurt your ability to remember just as much as the other villains. When he's around, we are distracted and forget to relax and focus. We feel like we are *finally* here: the big test or big game. At last! That takes our mind off what is most important. Then Mr. Overexcited laughs because he has won!

Keep Mr. Overexcited away. Stay relaxed. Use the **Relaxation Breathing Exercise**.

The Demotivator

He doesn't look like much, but this is one of the biggest, meanest villains of all. We are all visited by him from time to time. We think, "I'll never use this again." "I just don't care." "This doesn't interest me at all." "I'm not good at this - I shouldn't even try."

The Demotivator saps your strength and enthusiasm. Here are three ways to defeat him:

1. Picture yourself doing well at the activity. Visualize everything going well, then get started.

2. Trick yourself into wanting to learn or do well. I picture myself as a superhero. Whatever I am learning is the *exact* subject that will save the world. It's ***The Memorizer!***

You can be The Memorizer too. Make the scenario so silly that you are laughing at how crazy it is. Who would need to know these spelling words to save the world? Or be able to say this sentence in another language to sneak into the mad scientist's laboratory? It works, though, so try it!

Throughout this book you've practiced imagining things, so this should be easy. Making any school subject more fun with your creativity and imagination is simple. Use it to motivate yourself now!

3. Treat yourself. With your family's permission, get a bag of your favorite snack or candy. They should be small, like M&Ms or Skittles. For a healthier choice, use crackers, grapes or raisins.

You get a treat every time you do a small piece of what you don't want to. Answer a homework question? Get a treat. Read a paragraph in the textbook? Get a treat. Only one treat per question, paragraph or piece of work. Still not enough incentive? Get a treat just for reading the question, or opening the book. Get another treat for *thinking* about the question before you answer it. Get another one for *writing* the answer! Reading? One treat per sentence is fine if you're struggling.

Instead of candy or snacks, try this with pennies, dimes or quarters. Talk to your family about your struggle with The Demotivator and ask for help. Ask for your allowance, a bonus or a gift, but in the form of pennies, dimes, or quarters. Have them put the money in a jar or bowl. It's *their* money in *their* bowl. Have an empty jar or a bowl for you and *your* money for when you reward yourself with one coin per question or sentence.

It's amazing what happens. Suddenly, because of this game, you find yourself more willing to do the work.

The last way to defeat The Demotivator is my favorite.

The 90-Second Tool

Whatever you don't want to do, start it with the understanding that you can stop after 90 seconds. After 90 seconds, keep going... at least for another 90 seconds. After 3 minutes, I bet you will be able to continue. Defeat The Demotivator by *starting*, even for 90 seconds.

They seem powerful, but don't fear the villains. Knowing about them allows you defeat them. Use the tools, especially the breathing exercises, to make sure your memory stays strong!

List the top three villains you struggle with:

1.

2.

3.

List the techniques and tools you can use to defeat them:

1.

2.

3.

If you still struggle, talk to a teacher or family member. They can help.

Chapter 14

This Is Only the Beginning

Don't stop now.

You have learned some amazing tools as you've read this book. My hope is that you *practiced* them while reading. Knowing how to remember better is good. Being able to remember better is amazing. Fun practice gets you there.

Try every tool. It takes some time to learn them in the beginning, but once you do, you'll be able to learn more, faster and easier.

You are near the end of the book, but you are beginning a journey towards unlocking your amazing memory even more.

What's Next

Apply what you have learned by using these tools when you study. Use this book while you learn your vocabulary words, spelling, foreign languages, dates, math and more.

Keep using the three **keys** (**Picture**, **Connect**, **Review**) for everything you learn. If you have trouble, review the book and see if you missed something the first time you read it.

Think about the three **steps** to memory (**Get**, **Store**, **Recall**). If you have trouble, figure out which step is tripping you up. Use that knowledge to decide which tools to use to improve.

General Tips to Aid Memory

• What is your motivation?
It's easy to do fun things. Our motivation is that we enjoy them! What motivates you to do the things you *don't* like? External rewards, like positive feedback from friends or family? If so, ask someone for their encouragement when you do well.

Do you enjoy competition? Challenge a friend of classmate who is at a similar level. Who can get a better grade on the test?

Is the promise of a favorite treat (ice cream sundae or pizza party) enough to get you motivated?

Or are you motivated by internal rewards? Think about how good you'll feel when you **accomplish** something ("**acc!**").

Find a motivator and use it to get difficult things done.

• Step #1 of remembering: Get the information.
Many of the tools in the book work well in part because they force you to look at the information more deeply than you have in the past. They make you think about what you are reading and what you want to remember. If you are still having trouble, spend more time improving your focus.

• Quiz yourself.
Scientists are finding that one of the best ways to review is to quiz yourself. Take a practice quiz, work with your best friend to ask each other questions, or have your family read questions to you. You will be using the **Review** key to make those silly images even more memorable.

Congratulations! Well done!

That's it, you're done! You have worked hard and have successfully learned all about remembering. You have unlocked your amazing memory!

If you are still having trouble, free on-line coaching is often available for students (with a supportive adult family member or teacher). Visit www.featsofmemory.com for information. There you can also see more tools, get support, have your questions answered and share your successes.

About the Author

Brad Zupp is a professional speaker, entertainer and memory coach. His interest in memory improvement dates back to his childhood, trying to find better ways to remember information in school. In his 20s, Brad became fascinated with techniques that would allow an ordinary person to memorize a shuffled deck of playing cards, long numbers, or even an entire magazine. He learned the techniques and applied them to learning to speak a foreign language.

Several years later, he threw himself into learning more about the mind and memory, and soon after started attending memory competitions all over the world. (He has won several bronze medals in the USA Memory Championship.) Brad continues to improve his memory daily, memorizing decks of playing cards, numbers, names and faces, poetry, and more.

He speaks frequently on the subject of memory improvement for students in grades 3 through 8, as well as for senior citizens, baby boomers, salespeople and executives.

Acknowledgements

My thanks go to the memory experts who came before me, both thousands of years ago and more recently, for paving the way.

Thanks to Beth, my best friend and lovely wife, for her constant support and inspiration.

Many people helped with the rough draft of this book, and made it better with their thoughts and notes: Millie, Mary Beth, Martin, Aicha, Beth, Sofia, and Olivia.

To my readers, thank you for your interest and willingness to do (fun) work to unlock your amazing memory, and I wish you the best of luck!

Credits

Cover: Marko Tomicic, Julien Tromeur
1 Monkey Business Images
2 Constantine Pankin
2 Suzanne Tucker
3 Eric J. Strong*
3 Eric J. Strong*
4 ayelet-keshet
4 RomanYa
5 jonipangeran
6 Javier Brosch
6 alexwhite
6 Julien Tromeur
7 cobalt88
8 Lightspring
8 BeRad
9 Thodoris Tibilis
9 AlexeyZet
9 Marcio Eugenio
10 Julien Tromeur
10 Marcio Eugenio
10 Thodoris Tibilis
10 Lightspring
10 AlexeyZet
11 jonipangeran
11 marekuliasz
12 Fazakas Mihaly, DVARG
12 silroby80
13 cTermit
13 silroby80, cTermit, Andrey_Popov
13 Jason Swart
13 amasterphotographer
14 dedMazay
14 silroby80
14 dedMazay
14 amasterphotographer
15 Gorban
15 silroby80
15 dedMazay
15 yskiii
16 dedMazay
16 Eric J. Strong*
16 Sujono sujono
16 amasterphotographer
16 Eric J. Strong*
17 Eric J. Strong*
17 penang
18 alexwhite
19 silroby80
19 dedMazay
19 lineartestpilot
19 DVARG
19 Ron and Joe
19 dedMazay
19 dovla982

19 dedMazay
19 Fabio Berti
20 dedMazay
20 Karen Katrjyan
20 amasterphotographer
20 Matthew Cole
22 amasterphotographer
22 Eric J. Strong*
22 silroby80
22 Fazakas Mihaly, Johan Knelsen
23 Fazakas Mihaly, Ilona Baha
24 Fabio Berti
24 amasterphotographer
24 silroby80
24 Fazakas Mihaly, Johan Knelsen
24 Fazakas Mihaly, Johan Knelsen24
24 Fazakas Mihaly, Ilona Baha
24 Fazakas Mihaly, DVARG
25 Jonard Laganson*
25 Christian Delbert
26 Jonard Laganson*
26 Matthew Cole
27 ra2studio
29 Hibrida
29 Complot
29 Anton Vakhlachev
30 Matthew Cole
30 jorgen mcleman
31 Julien Tromeur
31 cobalt88
32 VectorShots, amasterphotographer, VectorShots, dedMazay, Kurilina Tatyana Andreevna
33 SFerdon
33 VectorShots
34 penang
34 dedMazay
35 Kurilina Tatyana Andreevna
35 penang
37 Javier Brosch
37 Sergey Nivens
37 John T Takai
37 milo827
38 Andrii Muzyka
38 Everett Collection
39 Julien Tromeur
41 Irina Rogova
42 RTimages
43 Julien Tromeur
44 Matthew Cole
45 Lorelyn Medina
45 RAStudio
47 Julien Tromeur
48 alexwhite
48 HitToon.Com
49 Matthew Cole
50 Julien Tromeur
50 Ron and Joe
50 Cory Thoman

51 M. Mandarano
51 HerArtSheLoves
51 Vladimir Bochko
52 Dirk Ercken
52 Lindwa
53 Artisticco
53 alexwhite
55 Michael D Brown
56 Julien Tromeur
57 Diana Taliun
60 SilverStand
60 alexwhite
61 Regissercom
61 alexwhite
62 Esteban De Armas
62 luchunyu
62 mj007
62 alexwhite
63 Javier Brosch
63 Opka
64 Julien Tromeur
65 Zarja
65 StockThings
66 Toponium
66 Javier Brosch
68 savageultralight
68 Ron and Joe
68 bazzier
68 Sarawut Padungkwan
68 patrimonio designs ltd
68 Matthew Cole
69 Teguh Mujiono
69 Azuzl
69 Sujono sujono
69 Javier Brosch
69 Miguel Angel Salinas Salinas
70 Jake Vicente, MaKars
71 Webspark
71 jehsomwang
71 alexwhite
71 yukipon
73 jonipangeran
73 Vitezslav Valka
74 Lightspring
74 Julien Tromeur
75 Danilo Sanino
75 Sarah Holmlund
76 Reno Martin
76 Julien Tromeur
77 GraphicGeoff
77 Anton Brand
78 Julien Tromeur
79 alexwhite
79 Arkela
82 Julien Tromeur
82 Julien Tromeur
83 PiXXart

Printed in Great Britain
by Amazon